W9-AWI-962

WE
THE PEOPLE
JANE ADDAMS

Published by Creative Education, Inc. 123 South
Broad Street, Mankato, Minnesota 56001

Library of Congress Cataloging-in-Publication Data

Klingel, Cynthia Fitterer.
  Jane Addams.

  (We the people)
  Summary: A biography of the wealthy woman who realized
her ambition to live and work among the poor and founded
Hull House, one of the first social settlement houses in
the United States.
  1. Addams, Jane, 1860-1935—Juvenile literature.
2. Social workers—United States—Biography—Juvenile
literature. [1. Addams, Jane, 1860-1935. 2. Social
workers] I. Title. II. Series: We the people (Mankato,
Minn.)
HV28.A35K55 1987   361'.92'4 [B] [92]   87-27152
ISBN 0-88682-165-7

WE
THE PEOPLE
JANE ADDAMS

HELPER OF THE POOR
(1860-1935)

CINDY KLINGEL

Illustrated By John Keely & Dick Brude

CREATIVE EDUCATION

JANE ADDAMS

Laura Jane Addams was born in 1860 in the little town of Cedarville, Illinois. A childhood illness left her with a slightly crooked back. She was a solemn, thoughtful little girl.

Jane's father was a wealthy mill-owner and a member of the state legislature. Jane, the youngest of his four children, was his favorite. Jane's mother had died when the girl

was only two. Jane admired and loved her father very much. He was an important and respected man. Jane was very proud of him. She often worried that she was not fit to be the daughter of such a fine man. She didn't need to worry, though, because her father dearly loved little Jane.

When Jane was eight years old, her father remarried. Now Jane had a stepbrother, George, who was her

age. They became good friends and had many adventures.

Although Jane enjoyed playing with George, she also liked to go with her father. One day, Jane's father took her on a business trip to nearby Freeport, an industrial city. The little girl looked with dismay at the dingy houses of the poor. "Why do they live here?" she asked.

"These people have no choice," John Addams said. "They are too poor to build nice houses like ours." Jane thought long and hard. "When I grow up, I will build a beautiful house. It will be right in the midst of houses like these. Then I will invite all the poor people to come and stay with me."

These were strange words for a

little girl! Mr. Addams laughed. But Jane never forgot that day.

When Jane was seventeen years old, she went off to school. She attended the Rockford Female Seminary. There she met Ellen Gates Starr, who would become her lifelong friend. During her years at Rockford, Jane earned the highest grades. She wondered what to do with her life. There were not many occupations for educated women in those days, aside from teaching.

Jane thought about the trips she used to make with her father and remembered the poor and suffering people she had seen. She had always wanted to help these people. Now, what could she do to aid them?

"Perhaps I could become a doctor," she thought. Jane decided that was the answer. Her work would then help others to live better lives.

Jane finished her studies at Rockford. She was twenty-one years old. That summer, her father died. Jane was heartbroken. She had a difficult time recovering from her grief. Then, one day, Jane went on a walk to the top of a hill. As she looked down upon the rooftops of the poor run-down homes, Jane realized how much sadness there was for so many people less fortunate than she. Jane realized that everyone must deal with grief, and that helping one another makes it easier. She would go to medical school and

train to be a doctor. Then she could live among the poor and help them.

That winter she entered the Women's Medical College in Philadelphia. She did well in her studies. Then her twisted back began to

cause problems. She had an operation to straighten her back. The operation was successful, but it left Jane nervous and unsettled.

The doctors recommended that Jane travel and relax. Her dream of becoming a doctor came to an end. Now what was she to do? She didn't like this feeling of uselessness. She wanted to help someone.

When Jane recovered from her

operation, she and some friends and relatives took a vacation to Europe. In London, she was shocked to see the poor people digging through the garbage in hopes of finding rotten vegetables.

In Germany, she saw weary women toting huge kegs of hot beer that splashed over and scalded them. She was told that their wages were 38 cents for a twelve-hour day.

Although Jane visited beautiful palaces and museums on her trip, she could not forget the hopeless faces of the poor that seemed to stare at her from every alley. They seemed to beg her to do something.

SLADE MEDIA CENTER

But how was she to help them?

After several years of aimless activity, during which she went home, then returned to England, Jane happened to visit Toynbee Hall. It was a new kind of institution—a settlement house. Dedicated young men lived in a house in a poor neighborhood. They had a library, taught classes, and did whatever they could to help the poor around them.

"This is what I shall do," Jane declared. Jane convince her friend, Ellen Starr, to join her. The two young women went to Chicago in 1889 to start their own settlement. The great city was teeming with poor people, many of them newcomers from foreign lands.

Jane met with those who were

familiar with the people of Chicago, and they told her where she could help the poor people the most.

In the midst of one of the worst slums stood a red brick mansion. It had been passed by the great fire of 1871. Flimsy cottages stood all around it. Garbage lay thick on the streets. Once this mansion had been the gracious home of a family named Hull. Now part of it was a warehouse and part was carved into tiny apartments. "It is the pefect place for our settlement house," said Jane. So they rented it.

Jane hired painters and carpenters to make the house a nice place to live. She and Ellen scrubbed and cleaned out the rubbish. With her own money, Jane bought beautiful

furnishings. She persuaded her wealthy friends into sending things for Hull House, too.

The slum people were amazed that "fine ladies" such as Jane and Ellen would want to live among them. They did not understand Jane's plan.

Jane and Ellen went to call on their neighbors. They began their careers of service by babysitting for working mothers. Soon they had a nursery school. Young children were no longer sent to spend the day in the streets. Now they went to Hull House where they were taught cleanliness and manners.

Jane once said, "When we went to Chicago, we had no definite idea what we were going to do. We

hoped that by living among the people we would learn what was needed."

They learned many things were needed. There were only three bathtubs in the whole neighborhood. Jane installed several at Hull House, and then she persuaded the city to construct a neighborhood bathhouse. It was so successful that many more were built all over Chicago.

Another problem was garbage.

The garbage collectors didn't bother to pick up the garbage in the poor neighborhoods, even though they were paid to do so. This angered Jane. She worked calmly but firmly until city officials had the garbage routinely collected and the streets cleaned.

Jane and her friends did many other things, too. They taught English, music, cleanliness and games. They comforted the bewildered and the sorrowing. The poor people loved them.

Other dedicated women and men came to help Jane and Ellen at Hull House. They expanded into new buildings. They built playgrounds. Newspapers and magazines had articles about the good work

Jane Addams and her friends were doing. Other settlement houses began to spring up in other cities. Jane had invented a new form of service career—that of the social worker.

Not only did Jane help people be more comfortable in their homes and neighborhood, but she was concerned that they be treated fairly and not be taken advantage of. She saw small children slaving in factories. She convinced Illinois lawmakers to put an end to child labor. Other new laws protected women workers and made factories cleaner and safer places to work.

World War I began. Jane's heart ached for the innocent people who suffered war's horrors. Jane strongly believed that all people of all nations

needed to work together. She believed they needed to understand one another. This way, there might be peace. She and other women from many countries started the Women's Peace Party. They called for a union of nations, a means of working together to solve world problems without war.

   During World War I, peace was

not a popular notion. Jane's ideas were years ahead of their time. She was widely misunderstood. Some people even called her a traitor. Wherever people were oppressed, Jane tried to help. She was champion of voting rights for women, of better schools, of relief for the aged, the sick, and the unemployed. Her work at Hull House continued and was known throughout the world.

In 1931, Jane Addams received the Nobel Peace Prize. She was 71 years old. Ailing now, she still supervised work at Hull House and visited the children while continuing her work for world peace.

Now many poor black people began to come to Hull House. Jane welcomed them as she had welcomed immigrants. Despite her illness, she still tried to help people with their problems.

She was at Hull House until a week before she died on May 21, 1935. People of all races, nationalities, and religions mourned her death. But the work of Jane Addams, good neighbor, lives on in the tribute of a member of President Franklin D. Roosevelt's cabinet:

"Parents who want to develop the finest in their children will bring them up in the Jane Addams tradition and those so reared will be the best citizens of their generation—steadfast, neighborly, serene and simple, crusaders in the never-ending fight for a finer and better social order."

WE THE PEOPLE SERIES

WOMEN OF AMERICA

CLARA BARTON
JANE ADDAMS
ELIZABETH BLACKWELL
HARRIET TUBMAN
SUSAN B. ANTHONY
DOLLEY MADISON

INDIANS OF AMERICA

GERONIMO
CRAZY HORSE
CHIEF JOSEPH
PONTIAC
SQUANTO
OSCEOLA

FRONTIERSMEN OF AMERICA

DANIEL BOONE
BUFFALO BILL
JIM BRIDGER
FRANCIS MARION
DAVY CROCKETT
KIT CARSON

WAR HEROES OF AMERICA

JOHN PAUL JONES
PAUL REVERE
ROBERT E. LEE
ULYSSES S. GRANT
SAM HOUSTON
LAFAYETTE

EXPLORERS OF AMERICA

COLUMBUS
LEIF ERICSON
DeSOTO
LEWIS AND CLARK
CHAMPLAIN
CORONADO